Bob McCluskey

He WALKS *with Me Through the* MISTS OF TIME

His Love Inspiring My Heart to Rhyme

HE WALKS WITH ME THROUGH THE MISTS OF TIME
Copyright © 2013 by Bob McCluskey

Unless otherwise indicated, all Scripture quotations are taken from the King James Version of the Bible.

Printed in Canada

ISBN: 978-1-77069-842-0

Word Alive Press
131 Cordite Road, Winnipeg, MB R3W 1S1
www.wordalivepress.ca

Cataloguing in Publication may be obtained through Library and Archives Canada

Dedication

My earnest desire is to offer up thanks to God for the inspiration that initiated poetry writing so late in my life and which continues to quietly inspire. I do therefore dedicate this book of poetry to God.

I would, however, be remiss if I did not recognise the encouragement, patience, and constructive criticism provided by my Bride of three years, Agnes Mary McCluskey. Although I would spend the better part of each day closeted away at my computer while leaving her to her own devices, she never complained. It is to her as well that I owe a great big thank you and to whom also, I dedicate this book.

Although God has inspired some 800 or 900 poems up to this time, I feel that as my age creeps toward ninety, this will probably be my last published book. It will leave some 500 or so poems unpublished by me at least...maybe the kids will do something with them, eh! *Sayonara.*

A Great Big Heart

September 10, 2012

Man, a great big heart is blowin' up in me
A love for all my brothers in the world
I'm tellin ya, we'd better wake up and see
The love in Jesus's heart for the least of these

Can't you see the beauty in the soul of man
Jesus can, Jesus can
And we all will too with Jesus inside
In every man, in every man

Stop the hatin', stop the killin'
Every man's a brother if we'll all be willin'
To go back far enough, like Adam and Eve
Nothin's too difficult for Jesus to retrieve

C'mon, open up, don't let fear overcome
Do something nice for a stranger
Love on everyone
Then you'll be like Jesus

Then when everyone is like His Son
Won't the Father feel grand
And peace on earth has now become
Just the way God planned

Ain't Love Grand?

May 25, 2011

There are men we hear profess undying love for God,
but how to describe.
How can one love a Lover so removed from any other,
unlike one's love for Mother or for a gentle, blushing
Bride,
what e'er betide?

We all understand, I do believe, sweet, fulfilling human
love, at least, I hope so.
For to love a lover, oh so fresh, one of human blood
and flesh,
requires no effort of intent, it does spontaneously flow,
don't you know.

With some men we are familiar, much in love with
avocations,
which do greatly edify.
If architecture is their passion, scrapers of the sky they
fashion,
or create fancy barns for pigs, which on farms are
called a sty,
I wonder why.

But now I fully understand why sweet love from God exposes
Satan's contraband.
Love must come from our Creator; God is love's initiator,
with surrender of our will, God's response was ever planned,
Ain't Love Grand?

Chosen by God

October 18, 2012

Who can know God; oh some say they do
and in different ways I suppose they might,
but not like we know our wife or our friends.
We know Him from the Bible word pictures,
which portray Him in all His infinite variety,
and sometimes even by a spiritual experience
when a merciful God chooses to wake us up.

In my unresponsiveness, God did that to me and
for me at fifty years of age because God knew
that I was just not getting it on my own. God
turned my life around then and I have tried,
however modestly, to endeavor to please God
by telling people, one on one, about Jesus.

On the other hand, I have known men, a few,
who, once they came to know God in their youth,
devoted their whole life to serving God;
not by just believing and obeying God,
but by studying and literally serving God
as Pastors, and later as Pastors of Pastors.
They faithfully followed a path in life that enabled
them
to ultimately influence many more people for Jesus
Christ,

but we must leave this with God...God knows!

And finally, I'm reminded that God's word speaks to all of this
in a way that gives me, and would give others I know, great comfort.
In Matthew 22, "For many are called but few are chosen";
and in John 15, "Ye have not chosen me, but I (God) have chosen you";
and in Ephesians 4, God says He gave to the church, some pastors, etc.,
which led me to conclude that my friends were given to the church by God
and that all we members of God's flock were each given to our families,
friends, and acquaintances to be witnesses for Christ to the glory of God.

Angelic Beings

September 13, 2012

Could we but see with eyes turned to God,
great wonders would come into sight.
Elisha revealed that the angels of God,
countless in number, not given to slumber,
in the night, were broadcast abroad.

The reason you see, for our problems
is we, do only give mental assent
to these angels who guard us
from the one who bombards us,
with dastardly evil intent.

The air I presume, in each other's room
contains angelic beings content
to surround us, on guard,
they don't have to work hard, to
the devil's device, circumvent.

Angels do surround us, fear's sent to confound us,
we really must learn to dismiss
the lies sent to conspire
from Satan, that liar.
Angels help when we learn to resist.

Clarion Call

June 11, 2012

Bewildered stood I
in God's brilliant truth,
electrifying this middle-aged youth,
that blinding flash
like shattering glass
descaling my jaundiced eye.
And I leaped with a yell
as deception fell,
a sinner all tattered and
headed for hell, never
more now to die.

Freed from the bondage deception gives,
because He lives! He lives! He lives!
to heal sick hearts with His love.
He severed my bondage
to stinking pride,
blowing open hypocrisy's
portals wide,
now it's Satan's turn
to cower and hide,
I'm headed for heaven above.

And if I were you, I would bend an ear,
pay close attention to what you hear,
God's message, unqualified love.
You know it's a ringing clarion call
to all infected by Adam's fall,
if you have any common sense at all,
you'll respond to Christ's message clear.
God made it simple for you and I,
let Jesus be Savior before you die,
don't submit to that tyrant fear.

Another World

February 4, 2011

Some men would feign with richest word, describe
God's universe so grand.
So eloquent with rhyme and line,
with soaring syllables so fine,
intellectual command.

And so would I, if I but could,
with stunted speech
and stunted intellect like wood.
Alas, I humbly now beseech,
such heights are far beyond my reach.

But then, thought I, cast down thine eye,
down into yonder leafy glen.
Observing life, the lowly Fly
seems much more talented than I,
knows just exactly when
to launch himself into the air, as
danger threatens near. Escapes my
footstep by a hair,
but trapped by Spider lurking there
in spider web, I fear.

This microscopic world below,
tumultuous with strife.
So worthy of our care you know,
as tiny creatures come and go,
entrancing, dancing, life.

Another world we seldom see,
designed by God's perfect plan.
These creatures so adaptably,
Live with each other happily,
right under nose of man.

Cold Gold

August, 2009

Forbearing caring, fearing all
the trials of life that make us fall.
Press in my friend,
seek Savior's face,
or...not at all.

What then, dear friend,
whence turn thee now.
What force, what source,
how seekest thou
for strength to win,
to maintain pace,
or weaken...fall.

Of ruthless men, I've known a few,
to overcome, they're overdue.
I'll do it my way, on they're drawn,
by siren call.

Single-minded, focused hard,
none restraining, non retard,
as ruthlessly they make their case
to win it all.

Then what reward, life nearing end.
What doth it profit them, my friend
to win whole world, their soul offend.
Price will appall.

Eternity is pressing in,
repented not, their life of sin.
Narrow way avoided well,
broader way approaching hell.
Lifetime habits still embrace,
God will call.

Current Economics!

October 8, 2010

The news that I hear,
from our neighbour so dear,
that behemoth entrenched to our south.
Reveals truth economic,
that's almost atomic,
and it isn't just word of mouth.

As their economy sags,
those political wags
start "quantitative easing" en mass.
Injecting not millions
but multiplied billions
to forestall a stock market crash.

To their banker's delight,
working into the night,
printing dollars with never a care.
With no structure behind it
they're going to find it
diluted in value for fair.

Fannie Mae, Freddie Mac
careened off the track,
massive mortgages issued subprime.
To fulfill their mandate,

weak mortgages create,
that could not be repaid on time.

But the good news today,
they've discovered a way,
for a while to avoid the abyss.
All foreclosures suspend,
banks again will depend
on a government handout, such bliss.

We have no place to gloat,
it's important to note
that our countries are quite intertwined.
Our security's hold
must not be in gold,
but must rest in a Christ-centered mind.

Conscience

October 1, 2012

Six billion souls in the interim
twixt life and death cavort.
Each one though, has a place in him,
a sanctuary rejecting sin
where God wouldst needs hold court.

Though man seems never aware of this
as history would attest.
It's a place that rarely invades the news,
a place where a battle for life ensues,
where occasionally, man is blest.

A place where Satan and God contest,
where man's spirit strives for good.
Where sin endeavours to rule and reign,
where flesh justifies sin again and again,
just as Satan knew that it would.

Conscience, disturbing the peace of man
when e'er it's decision time.
The things I would do, I do them not,
things I should not, I at times forgot,
O' wicked man that I am.

Who wins or loses this battle royal
is not for us to assess.
Who rules with Christ or who goes below,
who overcomes, only God can know;
Pray blessing on all, God would bestow
and that everyone, God would bless.

Danger, God's Gonna Get'cha

September, 2009

Hey George... WHO AM I?
You're You!
Yeah, George, but WHO?
Well...you're Bob McCluskey.
No! No! No! That's not my question,
that's my name! I'm not insane?
WHO AM I?

Well, you're unique, just like everybody else.
No! No! No! That's silly, if I'm unique,
I'm NOT like everybody else, if you'll pardon the
squelch.

Well, you live in British Col...
No! No! No! That' still not my question,
That's where I reside, where I abide.
It's where I hide.

What was that question again?
You know... WHO AM I? This I really must pursue.
Perhaps the task I should really ask is... Who the hell
are you?

Don't answer that, let's just move on.
I'm crying out to empty space.
That wasn't nice! No, no, I don't mean you, George.

My existence must from reason be. I CAN'T MEAN
NOTHING!
There's so much unending space where I'm floating
free,
Too many millions of billions of heavenly bodies, and
none for me.
Ooh! That's so poetic...

*But I think you're going too deep, or maybe I'm going
to sleep.*
Forgive me for mixing my metaphors.
So let's get back, we've gone off track...
WHO AM I?

Okay, I give up... Who are you?
Quit kidding around, George, I'm serious.
I know that my existence cannot be just happenstance
My life must have more meaning than to happen just
by chance.
*Of course it has meaning, you were planned by your
parents.*
Yeah, but that's the simple explanation, it doesn't
answer my question.
*So, billions of people are planning kids, just adding to
congestion.*

But what if there really is a God,
and he sent me here to earth!
Now take it easy, Bobby boy, let's not get crazy here,
next thing, you'll read the Bible, I could lose my friend,
I fear.

I think I'll do what all my friends are asking me to do,
I'll go to church with them for answers, you come too.
Well...okay, but cover my back.

Creation's Mystery

June 12, 2010

Sweet blossom, so lovely, once only a seed,
a small seed with a secret inside.
Unseen and unbidden,
it's loveliness hidden,
but filled with much glory untried.

Information in code, such perfection,
creation's miraculous reign.
It's the essence of life, with
much energy rife,
manifesting again and again.

And the life that ensues, the creator will use,
fulfilling His purpose so grand.
That day will arrive,
I could still be alive,
unfolding exactly as planned.

Now the seeds that we speak are created by God,
the flowers, His children sublime.
Growing up to their place,
in the human race,
fulfilling God's purpose in time.

Perhaps God sees this earth as His garden,
where He's tending and pruning each day.
To each flower provide,
His sweet Spirit inside,
to perfect His grand garden display.

Darkness and Light

August 27, 2011

Men who do evil
Love the night
Where none
are around to see
In the daytime
Witnesses
Give them a fright
As they vie
For obscurity

Pity the day Life
ebbs away
Enter eternal night
Ushered into
Stygian dark
With never
The hope of light
Or spark
None so blind
Oh God, as we
Who would not see
God's mystery
Aright

Cross Out Disobedience

April 2009

Our problem with God, is not faith too weak,
it's disobedience, far too strong.
In Romans 5:19, hear the Bible speak,
about sinners, a numberless throng.

By one man's disobedience, many were made
sinners...we're numbered with them.
By the obedience of one, and the price He paid,
righteousness was imputed to men.

Christ did not go to the cross because
a martyr He wanted to be.
And everyone's hatred was not the cause,
'twas obedience...His humility.

Hundreds of people were hung on a cross, in
that era, no mercy give.
Only one could redeem from eternal loss,
sinless Christ, that we all might live.

And why did He weep in Gethsemane,
surely not 'cause He had to die.
But sin entered in, twixt the Father and Him,
my sin was the reason why.

So disobedience...the reason I sin,
the choices I make...I'm the boss.
Which God could see, down through history,
I'm the reason Christ suffered the cross.

Death in Three Acts

July 30, 2011

ACT 1

Death angel hovers, moving slow,
above the darkened house below.
Escorting angels, bid to wait,
outside by the garden gate.
These things are never quite precise,
as Satan waits to roll the dice
to snare a soul who's sinking fast,
must face eternity at last.
Teetering upon knife edge,
hesitant to make the pledge,
while Satan, vying for this soul,
his loaded dice begins to roll.

ACT 2

Who's this alighting from a coach
somberly, to house approach.
He seems to be a preacher man,
come contesting while he can
with Satan for this sinner's soul,
to bring salvation, preacher's goal.
With preacher's mouth close to his ear,
voice strident so the man might hear,

begins reciting Bible quotes to touch his spirit,
prays and hopes while Satan gloats.

ACT 3

The battle now is raging hot,
they see response, but then cannot.
But now behold, an eyelid flutter,
croakingly, his voice did utter,
yes, forgive me, Jesus.
Rejoicing now, surrounding him,
death rattle sounding from within.
Satan raging, cannot stay,
escorting angels take away
this spirit soul to God with them,
angel leagues rejoicing when
Satan lost, this day.

Defiant Mankind

November 17, 2012

Made in the image of our God,
man's creativity doth man applaud
as higher, wider, farther yet
man's architecture flies.
To pierce the clouds, to scrape the sky,
to bridge great chasms, flying high.
Testifying to man, creative in stone,
yet, defiance not in this alone.

Man's visionary aptitude doth magnify
his creativity, as in heroic art displayed.
Arrayed, with all the world a home,
amassed in Vatican of Rome
or all the world's abundant piles
of cities spread abroad for miles,
yet, defiance also not in this alone.

To venture far into God's mystery of space
with scientific aptitude endued.
To dare to rocket to the place
where very God displays His face.
Instituting man's resurgent fable
to build a modern tower of Babel;
To breach the heavens God calls home,
yet, defiance also not in this alone.

In medicine, with great research
to heal man's ills at last.
To kill diseases one by one,
to make all healthy, everyone. But
over here, a plague's defeat finds
popping up beneath our feet two
other plagues more virulent that
were not ever evident,
yet, defiance also not in this alone.

Creative man, defying all God's evidential truth,
displaying great imagination,
worships gods of his own creation.
Declaring very God is dead,
conclusion reached within his head.
Defiant speck of mortal dust without
a trace of truth to trust,
by Satan led,
yet, defiance also not in this alone

But coming soon, that fateful day
when God will cleanse all sin away.
Each monument to bring man glory
on earth, a zero inventory.
Each knee will bow, each tongue declare
that Jesus Christ reigns everywhere.
Choose you this day, whom you will serve,
choose Christ, your sin He did atone.
As now at last defiance dies, in Christ alone.

Don't Worry...Be Happy

June 2009

(You can read it in Genesis 37, 39, 40, 41)

Many, many years ago, out in the Middle East,
Jacob had a youngest son, who should have ranked the least.
But he was Daddy's favorite, that made his brothers mad,
he even had a many-colored coat...no, not plaid.

All day he'd play with camels, they sure had lots of sand.
The sun shone bright and hot all day; this lad was really tanned.
At lunch he'd empty sand from all his clothes outside the room.
If he brought sand inside, his Mom would chase him with the broom.

This favorite son named Joseph, was really not to blame,
he didn't ask for favor...by God's plan the favor came.
God knew that Joseph's brothers would sell him as a slave,
say he's eaten by an animal...this tale to Dad they gave.

He ended up in Egypt, in a prison cell that stank,
I wonder if he was aware, 'twas God he had to thank.
I imagine Joseph praying, Lord, if you can find a way,
pour favor out on someone else, I've had enough
today.

If I get much more favor, don't think I'll stay alive,
Lord, much more of this blessing, I doubt that I'll
survive.
Now, you know I'm only kidding, Joseph always trusted
God,
God had a plan to bless this man, I know you would
applaud.

God gave Joseph super power, to interpret Pharaoh's
dream,
Pharaoh took him out of jail, and washed him nice and
clean.
He dressed him up in fancy clothes, bestowed his
favorite ring,
and made him his Prime Minister, lord over everything.

So boys and girls don't worry if everything goes wrong,
trust in God, you'll get the nod, just sing a happy song.
Jesus has His eye on you, when feeling all alone,
this trial will pass, and then at last, He might call you
on the PHONE?
(God can even do that by telling someone else to
phone you to cheer you up)

Do We See Men in the Spirit

August 23, 2012

We see them in worst city slums,
back alleys, dumpsters, doorways,
human refuse, mankind's off scouring, scums.
Only God knows where, in light of day, they
disappear and hide themselves away. Whoever
would come close or touch in any way, these
derelicts, this riff-raff, dirty bums.

I know those words are harsh, but speaking truly now,
is that not how we think of them deep down, be
honest!
Who would touch them? I know who would and who
did,
let me tell you, Jesus did and indeed still does.
He did it to the man with leprosy, that ugly illness,
that caused fingers, toes, and even nose,
and what other appendages God only knows,
to fall off leaving ugly, weeping sores that repulsed
men,
as they most assuredly would, and indeed do, today.

And how could Jesus comfort them, He's in heaven,
isn't He?
Yes, but He also lives here on earth in Holy Spirit filled
men and women,

who dwell in Him even as He dwells in them,
they have become His hands and feet here on earth.
But why, you might ask, are there not far better
candidates for heaven?
Jesus explained this to us when He asked this question,
what shall it profit a man, if he shall gain the whole
world and lose his own soul?
Or, what shall a man give in exchange for his soul?
Jesus revealed to us in these two questions, this truth,
one man's soul is worth more than the whole world,
and that is how Jesus sees the least of us, He has no
favourites.
He sees in the Spirit, and that man's spirit did not have
leprosy.
Dear God, help us to see men in the Spirit, just like
Jesus.

Enoch

July 6, 2012

Come forth from out of the mists of time, Enoch thou ancient one,
thy father lived beyond nine hundred years.
As also lived Methuselah, thy hoary, ancient son,
whilst thou hadst but the shortest of careers.

Cut off in the prime of youth, three hundred sixty-five,
one moment very evident, next moment thou wast not.
Occupied with life no doubt, quite busily alive,
important though affairs might be, they suddenly did stop.

Oh ardent man of God, 'tis said that thou did'st ever please,
thy Holy Arbiter enthroned on high.
In recorded Bible manuscript, man cannot now reprise,
engraved in stone for man who's prone, to wrongly deify.

'Tis said thou walked with God, a quite earth-shattering parade,
before God willed to take thee from the earth.

'Tis said that God with thee wast pleased, a glorious accolade,
requirest thou from God, a second birth?

This earth that thou departeth, in such sudden seeming haste,
wast spared as yet, man's rank depravity.
All man's unrestrained pollute, earth not sufferest this waste,
enabling man's unheard longevity.

Wilt doubtless rejoice with raucous voice, earth's reconstitute,
restoring God's new heaven and new earth.
With all the happy sons of God, wilt undoubtedly salute,
when earth enjoys her brand new second birth.

Perhaps we all might dance with thee, in merriment uncontained,
be thine ancient legs not over crotchety.
As God surveys His handiwork with pleasure unrestrained,
we too must plan to be there, thou and me.

Destiny

June 2009

This race we run, the one begun
by you and me in life.
For me, 'twas many years ago,
for you, more recently I know,
for many millions more, short years suffice.

Circumstances seem to come,
as well as children, one by one.
We carry on, we reach some goals,
the years go by, our life unfolds,
for some the end, for others, just begun.

Short-term goals consume our thoughts,
the road we're following is fraught,
with difficulties, many ups and downs.
With head bent down we carry on,
preoccupied, we only long
to stay ahead of debt and not get caught.

When burden seems too hard to bear,
when no one really seems to care,
some seek escape in needle or in cup.
Then pressure's off, they even smile,
life seems joyful for a while,
but morning's harsh, it's torture getting up.

That iron fist in velvet glove,
will never substitute for love,
to give relief, a heavy price he'll take.
The road of life is littered by,
the carcasses of those who lie,
defeated, paid the price for pleasure's sake.

As Jesus tries to break into,
this prison suffocating you,
God's Holy Spirit's stirring in your heart.
Speak Jesus's name, that's all it takes,
God's Holy Spirit gently waits,
to make you free, if you will do your part.

Exchange Leaders

October 2, 2012

Just imagine if all of the peoples
in all nations all over the world,
feared not one another,
like sister and brother,
without banners of hate unfurled.

Every culture has some things in common,
like affection for family and friends.
We all need to be fed,
have a roof and a bed,
and for some of our elders, Depends.

So I'd like to present a proposal,
which would really I figure, bear fruit.
Initiate right away, without any delay,
a one year exchange that their mothers arrange
between nations, all kings to commute.

A sabbatical for every leader,
spend a year in another man's shoes.
Legislate in their nation without aberration,
considering others with kindly elation,
then each other they'd never abuse.

My solution supreme, there you have it,
should each mother of leaders agree.
Every land would have peace,
even England and Greece,
ratified, when Lord Jesus we see.

Eternal Glory

October 17, 2012

How enormous is living
The expectation of eternal life
In the afterlife that awaits
How boundless, how joyful
The glory of eternity
The known, yet the unknown
The eternal mystery that awaits
To explode into reality
In that moment of transition
When this limited existence
Is released into heavenly glory
When the shackles of earth
Fall away in that golden moment
We stand in the presence
Of Almighty God

Euthanasia Excerpt

Lord Byron

When time, or soon or late, shall bring
the dreamless sleep that lulls the dead.
Oblivion! may thy languid wing
wave gently o'er my dying bed.

Appendage
November 11, 2012

Dreamless sleep that lulls the dead,
perhaps would welcome an escape
were it but true, but if truth be led
by selfish wish that man might make
for Oblivion! For deception's sake,
twould lead one on a path fools take.

Suggesting man would ere be less
responsible for all that he,
indulging flesh with wantonness
rejected all that God would bless,
defy God with impunity.

Not so fast my lad, that cake you had
you cannot eat and have it too.
That languid wing that gently waved

If now ignored, it shall not save.
It's sent from God to bring remorse,
repentance as life runs its course
if wishes were horses, beggars would ride,
but beggars were lost, if before they died
Christ Jesus's deity was denied.
God is not mocked!

Eternity

June 2, 2012

There lies within
Man's single-minded heart,
this passion,
from Thy counsel
to depart.
While deeper still,
men suffer day to day,
Thy covenant,
commanded to obey.
For deep within men's hearts,
thou didst instill,
Thy Royal command,
obedience of will.
And if thou vouchsafe strength
to follow through,
my Lord I will,
submit my will,
to You.
For therein lies
thy answer to desire,
the surest way
to damp that raging fire.

For God so loved
this sinful world,
He gave.
to liberate,
not ever to enslave.
And so my Lord,
I give my all to Thee,
to heart enfold
Thy vast untold
eternity.

False Security

February 5, 2011

Old men the Bible says, dream dreams,
Then may it be, Oh, Lord, my lord,
my dreaming throughout heav'n careens,
for there you do abide, it seems,
where we might have accord.

May it then be, Oh blessed King,
my sinful mind You'd plumb.
Laid open, painful conscience sting,
my warts, my sins, my everything,
while I lay prostrate, dumb.

My sinful heart, Your presence cleans,
for You are ever kind.
My judgment could be in my dreams,
not when I die, as Your Word deems,
hooray for peace of mind.

But woe is me, God's truth must shine,
God's judgment's very clear.
I must prepare whilst there's yet time,
surrender and make Jesus mine,
ere judgment sealeth here.

Faith or Works

July 7, 2011

If I have faith
and have not works,
my empty faith is dead.
If I have works
but have not faith,
the opposite is said.

But, if I have faith
and also works,
my captive soul is freed.
I then obey
God's will today,
in word as well as deed.

Free at Last!

June 9, 2012

Free at last, from bones to drag me down,
I'll revel then in spirit's destiny.
In heaven's endless, wide expanse to drown
with angels, all of earth's complexity.

In just the blink of an eye, to travel far,
from galaxy to distant galaxy.
Rebounding over heaven, star by star,
through light-years in a flash of ecstasy.

To promenade with loved ones through the wide
expanse of all creation calling me.
They'll teach me how to dip and how to glide,
and even loop-the-loop exquisitely.

And when at last, exhausted from this spree,
my Lord will draw me home to settle in.
Then delegating my new job to me,
judging heaven's angels will begin.

Then after many eons have unfurled,
can't know how long, there is no longer time.
For change of pace, God then will judge the world,
adhering to His principles divine.

Many other scenes I know will then await,
like White Throne Judgment, Bible says must be.
Or Judgment Seat of Christ, a Christian's fate,
let fools as wise men meddle there, not me.

Fall Away

September 13, 2012

Am I really sold out for Jesus?
C'mon, what's the name of my game?
Am I settled and tried, with a fire inside,
under pressure, would I be the same?

I really don't know, how far would I go,
if it cost me, would I keep the faith?
One day when the rubber encounters the road,
would resolve melt away like a wraith?

And what about you, have you looked into
your heart, I mean looked really deep?
Are you sold out for Jesus, forever to stand,
when your tested, what faith would you keep?

We can't answer those questions, not you and not I,
we won't know until testing time comes.
Many would, Jesus said, in last days fall away,
pray hard that we'll not be the ones.

Life's Passing Parade

September 5, 2011

The passing parade of life has made
people watching, a pastime grand.
So many avidly strive for each cent,
unaware they're missing the main event,
that's happening under life's big tent,
the salvation that God has planned.

Why are we here on earth anyway,
just to try to stay alive?
Is that all that life was meant to be,
to be born, then end up in the cemetery,
maybe for you, but not for me,
I'll never believe that jive.

Why do you think you're uniquely made,
you're not just an animal too?
Don't believe that baloney, we came from apes,
preached by the humanists, sour grapes,
I would sooner believe in a Jackanapes,
of which I have heard from a few.

They say we all happened by accident,
our uniquely creative tribe.
I wonder where their intelligence went,

believing Homo sapiens would be content
with assumption, conjecture, and in any event,
to godlessness we would subscribe.

So let's get together, they'll think we're uncouth,
to raise our voices so high.
Let them find their solace in gin and vermouth,
let them look for the spring of eternal youth,
we'll settle ourselves on the Bible truth
that God is enthroned on high.

Fear Not, Jesus Is Near

August 2009

In the midst of the heat wave I come
as a gentle cooling breeze.
To succor each lonely one
each broken heart to ease.

In the hottest midnight hour
to a soul in the grip of fear.
Where Satan seeks to devour
take heart, Christ's love is near.

In the tepid heat of dawn
from a night of restless sleep.
To a soul whose hope is gone
this soul our Lord will keep.

In the breathless heat of noon
lies one who strives no more.
Will fly to Christ's arms soon
o'er heaven's celestial shore.

In the evenings stifling heat
lonely girl gave all for love.
Heart repented, Jesus meet
all made new, by God above.

In so many places, stark,
in this world so filled with fears.
God sees each repentant heart
each repentant cry, God hears.

Come unto me, all ye that labor and are heavy laden,
and I will give you rest.
Matthew 11:28

Global Allegiance

November 7, 2011

We live on a great big ball of a world
That is spinning madly in space
My tribe lives here on this side of the world
While your tribe's on the opposite face
I believe this and you believe that
Is the twain ever going to meet
If the world was blown completely from glass
We'd be looking at each other's feet
We possess this and you possess that
And since we are stronger than you
We just take your "that" to add to our "this"
Though it's not the right thing to do
But we're stronger and do it anyway
Then we learn how to justify,
But if you were stronger and did it to us
We'd be praying and wondering why
Then you move over here and we move there
But you often don't integrate
You stay by yourselves like you don't really care
And then one of us starts to hate
But I just realized, and I'm really surprised
We do exactly the same thing too,
When we move en mass to your side of the world
We will not integrate with you

Maybe one day we won't think that way,
Out of prejudice maybe we'll climb
It would be nice with no prejudice
Perhaps it just needs some time
Oh, I know godly men went as missionaries,
But for others 'twas only a cloak
When promoters cheated the people there,
Christianity went up in smoke
To your side of the world is where Jesus came,
To your tribes that existed there
You exported Christianity around to us
Though you didn't know we were there
More importantly now as we're nearing the end,
When so many men are now lost,
Since Jesus died for the whole world too,
We must pray for all men, at all cost

First Nation Peoples

November 5, 2010

How many hidden, unvisited places,
where mossy rain forests fall down to the sea.
Where soft lapping waters reflect the wild faces
of hungry behemoths who fishing there, be.
The great bears.

How many gravelly wilderness beaches,
caressed by the fog, on some grey, dripping morn,
have witnessed the great shaggy, shadowy movement
of
beasts of the forest, whose litters they've born.
The great wolves.

As the great western ocean assaults their
escarpments,
their coastal defenses of granite and stone,
how many brave travelers, first Nation's warriors
have ghosted here silent, unseen and alone.
The great First Nations.

How many numberless First Nation's people,
untold eons before eastern civilized man
intruded so rudely with muskets and sickness,
decimating, destroying, as only we can.
The great conquest.

How many dignified clan leaders and elders
saw their children removed at so early an age.
Leaving villages empty of children and future,
motivated by nothing but alcohol rage.
The great experiment.

How many children uprooted, no culture,
removed from the land where God said they should
be.
No longer First Nations, but not white faces either,
with their culture destroyed, what hope could they
see.
The great confusion.

And now, how many children from resident schools
are grown lacking direction, many feeling the shame.
Alcohol desperation, mind-numbing, defeating,
having no place or culture designed to sustain.
The great destruction.

And now, their children also, on government dole,
live a smothering, meaningless, purposeless life.
Their whole culture, intended to nurture, sustain,
now so empty, child suicide's fast become rife.
The great genocide.

But, what is the hope we're beginning to see,
how many faint lights now beginning to swell.

How many First Nation's people are rising,
how many First Nations are now doing well.
The great hope.

How many First Nation's men, women, and children
are beginning to shake off the shackles of time.
How many First Nation's new Christians are standing,
Spirit guides to their people, revival sublime.
Their great salvation.

Gluttony Repealed

April, 2009

God, His infinite wisdom revealed,
when He first created man.
Making body first, from the dust of the field.
"Make his spirit first," we would have appealed.
But God's reason for this, He kept concealed,
when creation first began.

Consequently God did, in Corinthians' post,
that our bodies are where He will live.
Your body is the temple of the Holy Ghost.
We think He should live in our spirit, the most,
or smart mind, which betimes, executes a riposte,
but His reasons, God doesn't give.

Then, if God says it's so, we had better agree,
and be sure His temple's kept neat.
We improve our minds...books in library see.
Exercise for our spirit...biblically.
But this temple, our body, is exercise free,
and not helped, by the stuff we eat.

God knows, as it grows, this body we'll need,
if we're planning to hang around.
God wants us to change, with utmost speed.
Oh, God, please forgive us, and use us, we plead.

Then we'd best avoid gluttony, cut out the greed,
and shed that extra pound.

So, Lord, I repent, to the storehouse I went,
a few too many times.
I'll stay healthy so I can pay the rent,
having no desire, to live in a tent.
Radical surgery, my greed underwent,
now I'll save my nickels and dimes.

Forever and Ever, Amen

September 6, 2012

When a healthy, relatively young
body is completely immobilized
by a stroke, it's much more than
a stroke, a stroke sounds too gentle.
It is a cruel, battering assault on the spirit
and soul of that person, which changes
only the body, the essential person
remains the same. He might object
but does so silently. He might even scream
in frustration but also does so silently.
The most personal, intimate bodily
ministrations must be performed
by someone else as they will.
Helpers must be paid and though
they mean well, they are dispassionate
and detached by the very nature
of their humanity and will demonstrate
varying levels of attention, often dictated
by their busy case load. An excruciating itch
must remain excruciating until it subsides
of it's own accord. Other examples
of that person's agonizing imprisonment
are too numerous to be imagined here.
How long, if ever, until He might find
the only release possible, the peace of God.

Until he might develop that inner acceptance,
that ability to just let go and let God.
Forgive us, oh God, for our complaints
over comparatively trivial infirmities
and set these sufferers free in their spirits,
forever and ever, Amen.

God Bless the Little Children

September 30, 2011

Ah, the lovely little children
As they toddle to and fro
With skin so fair
And golden hair's
Reflected silky glow

And when caressing baby
With sweetest newborn scent,
We dream of God's elixir
Imbued when God injects her
With a spirit of content

But when I stand beside her
And then cast a wary eye
On my humps and bumps
And ugly lumps,
I often wonder why

My youthful vim
Has grown so thin
And I have a bleary eye,
And my blotches appear
Like banana skin,
It's enough to make one cry

While kids blithely leap,
I can hardly creep
It's very easy to see
That they're full of life
While I suffer strife
From my crotchety Gimpy knee

But never mind
God is ever kind
Everything God will renew
When I dance with Him,
Full of vigour and vim,
I'll again be that way too

For What Shall It Profit a Man

April 15, 2012

Dear, Lord...
You are by far the better friend
than any man might find.
As through life's tortured way we wend,
to come to Your determined end
with perfect peace of mind.

And may it be, dear, Lord, that we,
may not defy Your will.
But as You cried before the cross
not My will, Lord, but Thine.
May we rejoice to suffer loss,
that in Your book with bold emboss
our names emblazon time.

For what would profit man's amass
of all world's cankered gold.
If through the years his soul decay,
if on life's termination day,
they take his gold and God away,
just as God's Word foretold.

Heavenly Mystery

October 28, 2010

Have you ever wondered what we'll do in heaven,
eternity takes a lot of time they say.
If I'm a neat freak here on earth,
will I vacuum up for all I'm worth?
Will I be sweeping all those dark clouds far away?

Do the corners get quite dusty up in heaven,
do the bed sheets ever need a weekly change.
But if the washer has no soap,
our weekly wash would have no hope,
dirty sheets on mansion beds would seem quite
strange.

Some people think their cats and dogs will go to
heaven,
but whatever would those little rascals eat.
That litter box on earth was fine,
but who will clean it all the time,
above all else, we'll have to keep our mansion neat.

Some people say we'll sit on stars all day in heaven,
cascading out cadenzas on our harps.
Perhaps a thousand years or more,
our poor behinds are getting sore,
they say those pointy stars can leave some awful marks.

Some say that Sunday happens every day in heaven,
but if last night and then tomorrow's all the same,
to be at church most every day,
will leave us little time for play.
But as one fellow said on earth, what's in a name?

But I just suddenly remembered, eternity has no time,
time's existence won't be reckoned anymore.
So there's no longer night and day,
we can't get tired anyway,
so we'll never have to hear each other snore.

Gift of Love

October 17, 2012

What gift bequeathed most surely
Reveals a father's love.
The gift of gold is the beggar's gift
While the gift of love
Is intended to lift
His children's hearts above.

This world mundane,
Which did remain
Just as it was until Jesus came
And taught us how to live

Oh, the gift of gold will last a while,
Will make us happy, will make us smile,
But will canker and rust and turn to bile
Unless we learn to give.

While the gift of love
Is the harbinger of
His children's eternal life
For God is love, the Bible says
And his children will join him
One of these days
In heaven with the Father of Days
Removed from this world of strife

Hopelessly in Love

May 20, 2010

A tale of heaven's blessing, now poetically unfold,
this tale I know, will fascinate your mind.
It started several years ago, in Surrey I am told,
when a lady prayed to heaven, if God would be so
kind.

This lady's name was Agnes Mary Martin, so it was,
and the prayer she prayed, you'll find hard to believe.
She asked if God would send a friend to visit her
because,
she now was lonely and long past the time to grieve.

Now I'll share a little secret, Agnes Mary wouldn't
care,
every time she prays, God always seems to hear.
My mind sees a room in heaven, angels working there,
called prayer central, where she comes through loud
and clear.

I see an angel rushing, Agnes Mary's prayer in hand,
marked "urgent," he delivers it nonstop
where God gives it top priority, first in all the land,
and then scans below to check the current crop.

The angel said, there is a guy, McCluskey is his name,
he just mopes around with poetry all day.
I could go down and zap him, he wouldn't know I
came,
God said okay, but tell him what to say.

So poor old Bob McCluskey didn't realize he'd been
found,
when he noticed Agnes Mary Wednesday night.
The angel sprinkled angel dust, and love joy all around,
and McCluskey's goose was cooked, without a fight.

They noticed one another, and were very starry-eyed,
and it wasn't long, he took her out for lunch.
Soon the wedding bells were ringing, she became a
blushing bride,
they'll live happily ever after...that's my hunch.

God Lives, I Live

December 8, 2012

God lives, I live
That's enough for now
What more seekest thou, my friend,
Thy mutiny dost God offend
As down life's pathway
Blindly wend
To other idols bow

Are you the "I"
The one and all
The center of the world
Not true, for billions other "I"s
Contend with you,
Your place despise
As life around them whirls

So give it up, you can't be king
You'd best cut to the chase
The only center, only King,
The one who's Lord of everything,
Is Jesus who is Christ and Lord
Contentment comes with true accord,
Give Jesus Christ His place.

How Can God Love Me

February 23, 2011

God must get little satisfaction
seeing everyone in action
from the vantage point of vast eternity.
The beginning and the ending
as through life each man is wending,
with sinful hearts exposed for God to see.

Though His love is never ending,
there's no point in my pretending,
for to God my life is just an open book.
I might think my sins are tiny,
but to God they're black and grimy,
however can He ever bear to look.

He really loves me, I'm assured,
it's stated clearly in His Word,
though it's difficult for me to know just why.
I really love God too,
and hate the sinful things I do,
I'll try hard to get it right before I die.

But as I reason in my head,
I now remember when I read,
that He sacrificed His only Son for me.
Since to Him everything is known,
Christ died for me ere I was grown,
He loved me throughout all eternity.

So now I clearly understand
this gift from God to me so grand,
salvation means a total change of heart.
It's freely given, there's no cost,
at last I'm found, no longer lost,
too soon I'm old, but maybe now I'm smart.

God On High

May 17, 2012

On high within the vaulted courts
of heaven's vast array.
God dispenses souls to earth,
a baby soul for every birth,
from heaven's home, away.

Each soul pristine, not ever seen
by man, but loved by God.
I wonder, would His heart be sad,
enthroned on high, our heavenly Dad,
to send each soul abroad.

He would know their destination,
the earth in its muck and sin.
Each day from heaven thousands would flow,
God very aware as He sees them go,
of the destiny each must win.

Yet despite His love, God ever endures
their release to fulfill His plan.
Many sons like His only begotten Son,
the image of Jesus every one,
perfect God, yet perfect man.

And God I know watching us below,
would weep over multitudes lost.
But the price decreed must ever be paid,
for the harvest freed, that great parade
of God's sons who counted the cost.

Thank God for His life so cruelly spent
to cleanse a sinner like me.
Christ's precious blood would renew us all
with a cleansing flood if we'd only call
for Jesus to make us free.

How Will God Find Me?

August 27, 2012

I was thinking some thoughts the other day,
'bout how everything will unwind.
When I come to the end of my earthly way,
will it matter what part of the world I stray
to be easy or hard to find.

Will God send an angel to fly me home,
not my body that goes in the ground,
but my spirit? If I die in some hidden place,
will my consort discover my handsome face,
or will I end up just floating around?

Some pirate might tickle me off the plank,
wrapped in an anchor and chain.
Some twenty odd fathoms down in the deep,
an appointment with Davey I'd have to keep,
and I'd never come up again.

Or let's say, in some jungle in Africa,
when my bucket I happen to kick.
I'm lying there deep in some jungle snake,
who swallowed me ere I could make a break,
to depart would be quite a trick.

Would my angel be able to find me there,
deep in the swamp and the gook.
I would not want to miss that celestial trip,
if I couldn't get out I'd be having a fit,
so how would he know where to look.

Okay, so okay, I'm just having some fun,
my connection with God cannot break.
It would not ever matter wherever I fell,
even somewhere in heaven or even in hell,
Heaven's Spirit connection I'll make.

God Opens Blind Eyes

September 18, 2011

Take time to reflect on the meaning of life,
slow down from the cares of the day.
Lay down the hammer, the chisel, the knife,
secret yourself from consuming strife,
by hiding your heart away.

And then undertake the important next step,
just relax and empty your mind.
It cannot stay empty for long, I agree,
but this step is important, you soon will see,
pay attention, for next you will find
that you must now obey a wise biblical writ,
to think on things that are pure.
Something that is lovely, think on it,
things that are honest and just, would fit,
also virtue and praise for sure.

On these things, as you meditate time away,
you will be surprised to find,
your heart on its own will begin to pray,
its deepest secrets to God in a way
that you would not ever consciously say,
as God gives sight to the blind.

I Sought Deliverance

October 22, 2011

Lord, your promises are very clear,
I claim them all without the slightest fear.
I read them in your Word and I delight,
appropriating all to calm unreasoned fright,
they're mine, they're mine, all mine.

The answers used to come, no hesitate,
but answers come less frequently, of late.
No change I've made, I pray them just the same,
I'm certain, for I always take great pain,
to pray correctly, always just on time.

And then I read a passage from a Psalm,
which taught me I was doing it all wrong.
Deliverance I sought so God would hear,
but Psalm thirty-four, verse four was very clear
I'm praying wrong, Oh dear, Oh dear, Oh dear.

The psalmist sought the Lord, not just the need,
this revelation showed my foolish greed.
And what a revelation, now I'm free,
my seeking is for Jesus, He's now everything to me.
Free at last, I'm free, I'm free, I'm free.

I sought the LORD, and he heard me, and delivered me from all my fears.

Psalm 34:4

God's Forgiveness

August 30, 2011

How deep, how rich is God's forgiveness,
how lovely, the love of Deity.
How undeserved, why would God so bless,
bestow such loving tenderness,
on so undeserving you and me.

The God of all glory, so high, so true,
who even would notice these specks of dust.
The existence of little old me and you,
then would deign to answer prayers so few,
from we who betrayed His trust.

God's forgiveness is such a holy thing,
King David's adultery, murder too.
With repentance, forgiveness for everything,
as He would for us, not just for a king,
He would cleanse and restore us anew.

King David's sin, God did not conceal,
the truth ever publicly shown.
Because David's repentance was heartfelt, real,
and a man of undoubted holy zeal,
Son of David, is Jesus known.

I know we can't fully comprehend,
what forgiveness really means.
The old sin is gone, it's all washed away,
as if it did not exist to this day,
as impossible as that seems.

And it's there for me, and it's there for you,
this is not a difficult task.
If we'll just invite Jesus Christ to come in,
God will forgive us and cleanse our sin,
all we have to do is ask.

Impossible

November 27, 2011

A perfect world
To love abound
Will never in this world
be found
till Christ resides
in every heart.

It would
more likely
ever be
that up in heaven
they might see
spirits trim
a Christmas tree
with angels
taking part

But God does know
the world below
with evil
set apart
Will one day
be prepared
by Him

for Jesus Christ
to enter in
to every
man a sinner
into every
seeking heart.

God's Vast Celestial Halls

What stirrings in God's vast celestial halls where
ranks of angels eternally await His bid, existing for
one purpose only, will of God, surveying vast
creation, in God's endless glory hid, then majesty
of Triune God descends
To grace creation's long anticipated,
New, unstained, pristine terrestrial sphere
And God said, let us make man in our image
From just the elements created here.
The words He spoke did then invoke
Assembling of man's momentous, dear
But lifeless body, lacking yet that part serene,
Man's spirit man, to be internalized, unseen
As God breathed into Adam's latent intransigence
The breath of life, he then became a living man
Amazing now, the fellowship that did ensue
Man walked with God together in earth's paradise
Unthinkable that man could reason at the boundless
heights
Required to reach rapport with God, yet then did
Adam
For at creation man was gifted to commune with God
Face to face as Adam did, the promise for us all
Fated alas, to descend into self-banishment
And by inheritance, the banishment of all men for
God's decree

In perfect wisdom did design a later day, a better way
Where man's image made unto God would then
include
The mind of Christ, a blood washed perfect conscience
clear
To then redeem the tragedy of Adam's foolishness,
Transforming men at that momentous time of time's
division
Potentially to walk again with God as likenesses
precise
Of His only begotten Son, a growing tide of men as
gods
Swelling to the culmination of God's design to love and
be loved
Perfectly by many sons cleansed from sin to walk again
with God
In His anticipated, perfectly reconstituted worldly
paradise

It Does Seem Strange

July 28, 2011

It does seem strange,
the more things change,
the more they seem to stay,
the way they were,
just newer sir,
but in the same old way.

Ways and means and
outside scenes, change
before our eyes,
externals do admittedly,
metamorphosis.
But people change
since ages past,
only in their size.

Those who lie
are liars yet,
and thieves
are stealing still.
The penitent
from heaven sent,
still struggle
with their will.

So I suppose
that's how it goes,
men's insides
never change.
When God's eternal
mercy flows,
men's hearts
will rearrange.

Hand in Hand

November 1, 2012

It happened many years ago
Thirty, forty, I don't know
Does it really matter here
A touch divine to open up
A muddled mind, a half-filled cup
When suddenly the sky appeared
The grass turned green, the things I feared
Came into focus, recognized
That made myself, myself despised
Life had a purpose, now I knew
The God of all creation true
Was real, I feel, I know Him now
He graciously revealed somehow
that somewhere up ahead there lay
Eternity with Him one day
And something else you need to know
There's lots of room for you to go
Let's go together, you and I
There's nothing much you need to try
Just open up your heart to Him
Then hand in hand, we'll enter in
You and you and you and I

Live Forever?

November 3, 2011

I'm not going to live forever
I considered it though, for a while,
My wardrobe, a major endeavour
When I think of it now, I smile
My socks, my shoes, my new tutus
Would be constantly changing style
And what of my friends and family
If they didn't decide to stay
I would have to renew, all of you too
Each time that you went away
And then I considered my physical shape
I'm appalled that I'm coming apart
How would I do in a decade or two
This could really be hard on my heart
So I don't want to live forever
Certainly not in a hospital bed
Even now it's a major endeavour
I already need a retread
So I'm not gonna stay and just wear away
I'm going to heaven instead

Hate!

January 7, 2012

The journey we're on from beginning of life,
until life drains out at the end.
A different adventure for every man,
observe it as God, if you ever can,
looking down on a world of strife.

All beginning as babes at their mother's breast,
each born to a different fate.
A hovel for some, others mansion blest,
each one competing with all of the rest,
being taught to selectively hate.

The blacks hate whites and the whites hate blacks,
and the Shiite's, the Sunni's abhor.
The Catholics and Protestants launch their attacks,
the poor everywhere seem to fall through the cracks,
while Jesus stands at the door.

One faction says Christ died only for them,
while another is chosen, they think.
Satan strewing division, hate and mayhem,
others say there's no God, never realizing when,
at God's judgment the horror they'll drink.

This tale up to now, speaks of nations and tribes,
and it's true, they've a judgment call.
But each man stands alone when God's judgment prescribes,
it's too late if our hate with God's goodness collides,
choose God's Love, Jesus died for us all.

Lord, Lord!

June 21, 2012

Lord, were I stricken dumb, a mute,
    or just a bush, a tree.
What ere Thy will designed to suit,
    I'd still bow down to thee.

Or didst Thou deign to make me fly,
    an eagle on the wing.
Yet even though majestic, I
    would stoop before my King.

Or were I but a warbling bird,
    a singer on the wing.
if ever it displeaseth Thee,
    I nevermore would sing.

Or were the seas to cover me,
    some twenty fathoms deep.
With my last breath, I'd do my best
    to praise Thee, ere I sleep.

Lord, in Thy image I was made,
    free will, my soul obeys.
Though in my flesh, I'm weak, afraid,
    I'll honour Thee always.

Lord, each and every word I said
came from the heart of me.
But please excuse my fasting pledge,
I think it's time for tea.

Hell!

February 26, 2011

"Eternal rest"...platitudinous drivel, there is no kind of
resting in hell.
If that's where we go, and it might be, you know,
it's a horror described very well.
I'm just the messenger, don't blame me, the Bible
description is clear.
It's a burning without ever being consumed, if ever
you enter, forever you're doomed,
and many have entered, I fear.
For the Bible describes the two ways we can go, the
choice being ours to make.
The road that's wide, where sinners abide, or the
narrow way for the saints today,
choose with care, which road you take.
To end up in hell when our years expire, an
unthinkable fate to endure.
We are then at the mercy of Satan's ire, in a
bottomless pit of unquenchable fire,
with great gnashing of teeth, for sure.

Jos 24:15 And if it seem evil unto you to serve the
LORD, choose you this day whom you will serve...

Heaven!

"Eternal rest"...now applies with delight, what a
wonderful place to "retire."
With the presence of God, in a setting so grand,
perfect rest at our Saviour's hand,
made free from eternal hell fire.
Our eyes will see the King in His beauty, enthroned at
the Father's right hand.
With endless delight we'll sing God's praise, in the
wonderful presence of Ancient of Days,
with music resplendently grand.
Uncountable angels in joyful assembly, fill heaven with
worship and praise.
From God's pure presence, His love will flow,
inundating the saints in worship below,
where the sheep of His pasture graze.
The witnesses compassing all about, will welcome us
in this place.
We'll meet all of the saints we used to know, who left
us behind in the earth below,
And meet loved ones again, face to face.

Jos 24:15 ...but as for me and my house, we will serve
the LORD.

Lost Eden

April 1, 2011

There is a place, a lovely place,
prepared by a heart of love.
A place where hungry, hurting souls
are nurtured from above.

A place prepared by God's design, with
death and disease unknown.
Where little children are loved and fed,
where every care is shown.

Where hatred and greed are alien,
where unkindness does not exist.
Where everyone's greeting everyone else,
with an open hand, not a fist.

Where the one true God is worshiped,
with love unfeigned and true.
A place prepared for eternity,
by our heavenly Father for you.

The Garden of Eden, God's perfect design,
where all man needed, grew.
But right at the start, God knew man's heart,
and started planning anew.

When man disobeyed the Father's command,
Satan caused him to sin.
He embarked on an independent path,
in a battle he couldn't win.

Down through the years, man's rebellious fears,
brought the consequence we now see.
Wars and sickness and hunger and thirst,
great destruction for you and me

God's ultimate plan, the redemption of man,
God proceeded to activate,
because we disobeyed, from the garden strayed,
thank God that it's not too late.

All the suffering then would not have occurred,
God's perfection would be the norm.
We kicked over the traces, to forfeit our places,
unaware of the gathering storm.

God knew all along, that we'd sing the wrong song,
but that later He'd give us a choice.
Choose Jesus, God's Son, He's the only one,
we must worship, and all with one voice.

So now that you know it, you mustn't forgo it,
just make that decision today.
Repent of your sin and invite Jesus into
your heart, restore Eden this day.

How Many Gentle Hearts

June 3, 2011

How many gentle Jewish hearts, how many broken
Jewish dreams,
baked in the heat of German furnaces, it seems,
incinerated only to sustain German racial purity,
where purity of hearts redeemed ne'er played a part.
How many classical fingers and brilliant minds were
broken
by men who that same night would bring their child a
token
of their love and tenderness, their guilt assuaged
perhaps
by love from wife and family.
And then tomorrow back to work, mindlessly to break
the will
and break the bone of gentle children coming out of
adolescence,
about to enter into the world of dreams imagined only
yesterday,
introducing their minds instead to madness too
obscene to think upon.

And so, to the question that burns inside of me, could
there ever, ever be
the slightest possibility, these men might find
redemption for their sins?

My flesh revolts when such a thought begins to rise
from my subconsciousness.
And yet, my spirit knows that God's Word will remain
inviolate. God's Word,
which undeniably proclaims that true repentance
always brings forgiveness.
How could this ever be, it seems impossible
and must be left to holier minds than mine.
But yet, upon reflection on all that God's Word reveals
of hell,
this eternal, burning agony that will not ever end,
must not await, not be the fate of any man, including
children's torturers,
my spirit shouts a loud resounding YES!
May God grant surviving Jews, grace ever to forgive
these men who also rank among those for whom
Christ died.
Christ's blood to cleanse repented sin cannot be
denied.
My compassion never will entreat within the range of
Christ's,
on whose compassion my redemption too, eternally
relied.
And so in summing up, I must reluctantly conclude,
that no one's judgment of another's sin, may e'er
intrude,
into the place where God alone must be the arbiter.
Oh, Lord, I pray, please find a way, to bring every living
soul, unto repentance.

Lottery of Life!

October 9, 2010

In the lottery of life we gets a number,
within the span from one to ninety-two.
If we only had our way we'd tear asunder
every limit, I know I would, wouldn't you?

Now, the number ninety-two is arbitrary,
and I know I shouldn't limit anyone,
but the thought of living longer's really scary,
at ninety-two, can anyone have fun.

Now, some numbers make recipients quite happy,
while others think their number is too small.
In the lottery of life, please make it snappy,
'cause your number's on that little bouncing ball.

But no one's fast enough to see their number,
so no one knows which day will be their end.
To find the mystery of life, you'd best not slumber,
you might awake to find you're dead, my drowsy
friend.

In the lottery of life, so many losers,
so many carelessly exist without a thought
of whether at the end there might be something,
a godly blessing, but so many just get caught.

So many pay their dues and takes their chances,
as if there's nothing they can really do.
But instead of death's destruction, they'd find glory,
if they'd worship Jesus Christ before life's through.

How Many Times?

July 28, 2011

How many billions of times in this world,
has man's journey of life played out?
From birth to death as each life unfurled,
how many curses at God were hurled,
how many would worship, devout?

How many traveled from birth to death,
defying Creator, divine?
How many fools have lived to profess,
that no god could exist for them unless,
he'd suspend the passing of time?

How many times has our Saviour revealed,
to the blind who will not see?
His love poured forth on the sick God healed,
or the sentence of spiritual death repealed,
whom His Holy Spirit made free.

Father, forgive them, Jesus prayed,
they know not what they do.
As He hung on the cross with back so flayed,
not for Himself was He ever afraid,
He was praying for me and you.

Who knows which day life's door will close,
better choose you this day, whom to serve.
When we come to our final resting place,
our reward, either condemnation or grace,
will be the reward we deserve.

Dry Bones
(1: Ezekial 37)
November, 1, 2009

When we've come to the place,
where we're down on our face
and the heavens seem like brass.
The world's fast closing in
don't know where to begin,
no response when we call,
we're beginning to fall,
down into a yawning crevasse.

When we earnestly pray,
to the Lord we relay
with great detail, the horror we're in.
Do we tell Him how sadly
we're treated so badly,
so completely unfairly
by them, that we're barely
alive, don't know where to begin.

Well, my friend, that's a prayer
that won't go anywhere,
be assured God has heard it before.
Take a lesson today

from what God had to say
to Ezekiel's surprise
when he saw all those guy's
dry bones on the desert floor.

All those bones where they lie,
they were dead, they were dry,
but Ezekiel obeyed God's command.
Spoke the word of the Lord,
then saw his reward,
they all rattled and stood,
like God promised they would,
God breathed life as they started to stand.

So obey God, get some sense
It's now time to commence with
faith, the solution to pray.
Your dry bones look like death,
but the Lord with one breath
if you'll speak it, can raise them,
but you must appraise them
restored, that's what you must say.

After that, when you pray
with great thanksgiving say
with rejoicing, you see it as done.

Now with God you agree
the solution must be,
you will no longer doubt it,
to the heavens you'll shout it,
with God, it will surely come,
see your dry bones starting to run.

If Jesus Showed Up

May 15, 2012

If Jesus showed up at our house today,
hungry and thirsty, what would we say?
Would we check Him out through the peephole first,
would His apparition elicit a curse
with an order to go away?

If Jesus showed up at our house today,
dressed in the Middle Eastern way.
This was His habit of course we know,
would we all stay quiet and hope He'd go
unobtrusively on His way?

If Jesus showed up at our house today
with a turbaned head and feet of clay,
would we be conditioned automatically,
a dangerous terrorist to see
and run the other way?

Or, if Jesus showed up at our house today
would we fall on our knees and begin to pray?
Would we dance with joy while embracing Him
with hugs and kisses and then begin
to entreat Christ Jesus to stay?

I like to think this is what we'd do,
but we'd need God's Spirit to see Him true.
None so blind as those who will not see,
so we'd best decide who we're going to be
before God's judgments ensue.

Man or Beast

December 17, 2011

Men manifest a high regard for mortal man's remains.
though flesh they say, is mortal clay which nothing
more contains.
A baby yet within the womb is not a human life,
yet they will place within a tomb, dead husband or
dead wife.

If mortal flesh does not contain reflections of our God.
why do they manifest respect, interring 'neath the
sod.
If man's remains are only clay, why treat them with
respect,
the elements contained within, they really should
collect?

Should render human corpses down for all contained
within,
all teeth and hair and outer wear, each placed within
it's bin.
Since man is only animal, and this they preach as fact,
the boundaries of our cemeteries, would rapidly
contract.

I know I'm speaking foolishness, your attention to collect,
as history evidences, funerals treat man with respect.
Regarding there a friend's remains, they feel a certain awe,
aware of something missing, unaware of godly law.

This is the key, at least for me, man's spirit holds man's life,
when spirit man escapes this flesh, to exit in a trice,
goes back to God who gave it, while flesh goes beneath the sod,
this is the truth my Bible tells, as evidenced by God.

And further, if we value truth, then judgment times await.
The Bible outlines clearly, every saint or sinner's fate.
While there's still time, dear friend of mine, you must rebellion sever,
confess your sin, invite Christ in, much better late than never.

Intentional Design

January 2, 2010

From elements, non ever seeing,
God spoke creation into being,
the glory and the beauty all now see.
For in His mind God had it planned,
each element, creation grand,
and put it all in place for you and me.

The heavens, stretching endlessly,
God determined they would be,
as well, the simple beauty of a rose.
Creation, whether great or small,
God's mind designed, then made it all,
everything sustained, while mercy flows.

This order some opine, evolved,
the wonders that keep us enthralled,
just happened right up to this very hour.
But if all by chance just came to be,
then here's a thought to you from me,
how come there's never been an ugly flower?

Monkey Face
June 2009

Some folks think they did descend
from monkeys in the past.
For some, could it be really true?
Now that would be a blast.

But that's not true for me and you,
the Bible says we're made,
in God's image...in likeness of,
our God we're all arrayed.

Don't have an Uncle Monkey Face
swingin' from a tree,
or a Hairy Aunty Mary,
they might say resembles me.

Some monkeys have prehensile tails,
ensures they'll never fall.
But poor ole' me it's plain to see,
ain't got no tail at all.

I resemble my creator,
that makes me creative too.
Did you ever know a monkey
who might write a poem, for you?

And monkeys are devoid of feet,
four arms, each with a hand.
No problem for our swinging friends,
their hands they use to stand.

I've heard that some would postulate,
if given lots of time,
a monkey at a keyboard could
create a lovely rhyme.

Let's say a million years or so,
just tapping at the keys,
this monkey dance create perchance,
a rhyming verse to please.

But my, oh my, that is a stretch,
if you should ever find,
a monkey busy writing verse,
to you I would remind.

He'd have to be much older
than Methuselah, without fail.
I'm sure if ever he showed up,
we all would grow a tail.

Israel, Start-Up Nation

June 7, 2011

Most everyone is unaware of influences everywhere
that analyse, philosophise, and then affect,
decisions made at levels high, improving interaction by
small nations that no one would e'er expect.
Like Israel, a start-up nation, causing neighbours'
aggravation,
while building a reserve of intellect.

Highly valued education is encouraged by their nation,
science favoured, engineering topped the chart.
When young people are careering, facing life with
great elation,
technology appearing to be the grand initiation
to the military, where they all must play a part.

Encouraging collective braining, in nurtured military
training,
teaching trainees all to think upon their feet.
Adapt as situations come, and this applies to
everyone,
if junior officers, a General ever meet.
Won't hesitate to criticise, if in an army exercise,
that General makes decisions indiscreet.

These men emerge from military, heroes extraordinary,
knowing how to innovate, to take a chance.
With venture capital on tap, and ingenuity a snap,
a start-up company with their brothers from the
service,
next on tap.

And if their start-up fail, no recrimination and no jail,
failure is regarded as a temporary stop.
Encouraged to begin again, financing easy to obtain,
they just keep on innovating, for the prize they know is
waiting,
at the top.

Most Important "I"

December 29, 2009

Why am I the center
of life's plan, who
do I think I am, who do you think I am? Do you
see me as central, or a
peripherally unimportant
man?

Or, do you see, this "me" at all,
this most important "I"?
What effort now would you expend,
to, from extinction apprehend
this world's
most centrally important guy.

But then I hear you say,
no, no, that isn't true,
all assuredly, relates of course, to you.
The world and all contained,
encircle you, you claimed,
a claim we all
pretend to all, eschew.

Now others I'm aware,
are thinking too,
that they're the most important,
much more than me and you.
This indulgence, that's expanding,
our attention now demanding,
absolution, a solution,
selfishly we'd misconstrue.

So who else could be so central,
if it isn't you or me,
to all bow down, proffer the crown,
elect him honoree?
Wow, my wisdom just awakened
as my ego I forsakened.
His name is Jesus Christ,
I once was blind, but now I see!

Israel!

May 29, 2011

A nation lying midst the dust of history,
hate her if you must, you will not hate alone,
though why's a mystery.
Born anew so recently, two thousand years
of waiting in the wings.
Her bloodlines yet securely kept,
despite persecutions so adept,
manifested by racial half-brothers
who propogate deceptions that by unspoke assent,
populate the newsrooms of the world.
The half-lies of deceptions ilk,
ingested with her mother's milk.
History's demonic serpent rallying,
in these last days to spread his evil coils
round this bloodied sliver of a land.
Recruiting brothers brainwashed into believing,
theirs is a most holy battle cry.
From north and south and east and west,
with slavering hunger to expunge
this hated insult of a land,
in the collective midst, a boil
that must be lanced, a sacred task they scream.
And come they will, with other-wordly hate
until, rank upon rank, her mountains inundate
with irreconcilable, rabid, genocidal hordes.

Then, with imminent destruction poised to strike,
God will arise!
Fire from heaven, on phalanxed armies falling,
men grinding tongues from pain, unseeing,
brother killing brother, fleeing
from consuming fire of heaven's holy rain.
Their blasted bodies covering bleak mountainsides,
Israel spending many months in burying the dead
scorched survivors fleeing back in scattered bands,
true peace at last will fill God's holy lands.
Fulfilling Bible prophecy, God's truth intruders feel,
Messiah now returned, forever more to cleanse and
heal.

Shed All Pretense

December 21, 2012

What passion burns within me
What truth lies buried deep
What care I, dare I, swear I
What destiny might keep
Alone

Come fly with me to the unknown
Shed all pretense, confess
Dare to stand against the tide
To be despised, to venture hide
And bone

Stand for truth as Jesus did
Defy the devil's horde
To hell with every liar then
Defiers of all godly men
Said godly men to never
Sin condone

Jesus Really Does Love You

August 22, 2012

I saw a woman the other day
As I sat in my car she wandered my way
She was skinny, careworn, when she bent out of sight
I looked out to see if she was all right
But with a few sighs, she straightened back up
With her wonderful prize, a cigarette butt
As she wandered away, I felt very strange
Down deep in my gut, my peace came undone
Was this all prearranged by the wonderful one
Who created us all, I just had to move
And hurried to catch her with nothing to prove
She stopped when I called and I felt out of place
I was not too enthralled by the look on her face
But I just had to tell her she mattered somehow
And the words seemed to come unbidden
I told her that Jesus was watching her now
And that nothing from Jesus was hidden
I said I was a Christian, and Christ loved her too
And He just told me, I must give this to you
He knows of your suffering, of all your remorse
He really does love you, and He is your source
She looked at the twenty with eyes opened wide
And her face brightened up, something happened
inside
He really does love me, she said with surprise

He really does love me, with tears in her eyes
He really does love me, as she wandered away
Truth entered her heart, she met Jesus today
Now someone might say, she'll just spend it on drugs
Tho I sensed true remorse when I gave her those hugs
She may or may not but that's not my affair
She'll be clean, when in heaven Christ welcomes her
there

Never Give Up

February 2009

God told Abraham, that Sarah his wife,
was going to have a child.
Not only was Sarah ninety years old,
but barren too...pretty wild.

He considered not, his one hundred-year body,
dried up like a barren clod.
Nor could Sarah's dead womb diminish his faith,
he was giving the glory to God.

Here I thought strong faith was for *getting* stuff,
but not in Romans four.
He was strong in faith, *giving* glory to God,
now, that's what faith is for.

But nine months later, Isaac was born,
and when fifteen years old,
God commanded that Abraham slay this son,
in Genesis we are told.

This command contradicted the nature of God,
who restored man after the flood.
God prohibited human sacrifice,
no shedding of human blood.

But God led him right to the mountain,
and he took his son to the top.
We notice he never told Sarah the plan,
she would surely have made him stop.

Isaac saw only, the fire and the wood,
so he questioned his dad, what's the plan.
Abraham prophesied, in Genesis 22,
God will provide *Himself* a lamb.

For God was in Christ, reconciling the world,
even unto Himself.
Out of the Father's bosom came,
the only begotten Son, God's wealth.

So now, coming back to that mountaintop,
on the altar Isaac was tied.
As Abraham raised his knife to strike,
his ears were still open wide.

Where we sometimes go wrong, we stop listening,
didn't God say, kill him now?
If we were Abraham, we might have proclaimed,
no devil can change my vow.

But because Abraham kept listening,
he heard God say, the knife he must drop.
So even after we've prayed, and heard from God,
keep listening...do not stop.

Love Came Down

December 10, 2012

Love came down to a world of sin
To be hated and vilified
But Love overcame
As Christ entered in
To a world of shame
That rejected Him
Who loved
Even ere He died

Love came down that epic day
God entered the world of men
In bodily form
That eventful morn
To take on flesh
As a baby born
To save the whole world
From Bethlehem

God's Love came down for eternity
God's Love came down to stay
God does not change
God never will
God's Love forever invades until
Every man by a glorious act of will
Is born again one day

New Life-Forms

September, 2009

We hear a lot of talk these days
where planets, if in many ways
were constituted just like earth,
more life-forms could arise.
Perhaps eliciting our mirth
with massive heads and beady eyes.

Some romantics live to see
away up in the heavenly
a planet just about earth's size
not frozen ice, but watery,
their hopes to realize.

What excitement would awake
in hearts of men if they could take
a light-years voyage into space
and then perchance to find a place
where lives an other-worldly race,
perhaps like us, they postulate.

Then if and when this did occur
are thoughts of riches premature.
To gather spoil, we'd go to war,
what else is exploration for.

But breaking through this foggy mist,
if other-worldly men exist
with spirits, souls, and hearts like us
who God is keeping there in trust.

Would they be saved by Jesus too
if living life with heart that's true,
or, not behaving very well,
will viewing us, become their hell.

Do you think we'll ever really know
space men observing here below
from spaceships flying up above,
Oh, Lord! We really need Your Love.

Lucifer

June 26, 2012

Incongruity displayed
Lucifer's consuming pride.
Full of wisdom it was said,
inordinately beautified.

Whatever did become of all
the wisdom he could laud.
To strive to sit on the sides of the north,
above the stars of God.

A vision indisputable,
he shone with all desire.
Created in God's crucible,
to walk on stones of fire.

The anointed cherub that covereth,
God had set him so.
Until God's eye uncovereth,
where iniquity did grow.

His beauty had seduced him,
he was filled with massive pride.
God cast him out of heaven for
the sin he held inside.

So this should be a caution
for all of God's mankind.
That sin of pride He'll not abide,
we hasten to remind.

He Just Can't

December 25, 2012

The devil can't be such a terrible guy
No one could be that bad
I have asked the question
I have wondered why
He can't just reform
He should give it a try
He might find
He's a kind sort of lad

He was after all, when created by God
The most beautiful creature extant
I've been wondering why
He won't give it a try
Make a clean breast of it
Make the best of it
Guess he would if he could
He just can't

So the point that I guess I am making
Just in case you were wondering why
We all, this advice should be taking,
Because Satan will sell us the lie
That our sin we can hide
Keep it hidden inside
God never will know

We are all good to go
With the canker that killed him,
his pride

So, deride if we will, but our sin's set to kill
If we fail to ask Jesus inside.

Hefty Headstones

December 18, 2012

Have you noticed how big the headstones used to be,
how solidly they insinuated permanence, immobility.
As if the loved one underneath might never leave us,
not while that solid block of granite held their name.
There was somehow, a reassurance and comfort there.

But a practicability has set in of late, reducing their
size
to a flat plaque of limited dimension and miniature
height,
enabling the groundskeepers to mow the grass
unimpeded.
Might we call this an invasion of our right to hold them
here,
or is that block of granite impotent to restrain them.

Could it be that there is manifested here a larger truth,
have we finally faced the reality that they have gone
on?
I refer here to the essential "they," the unseen eternal
"they,"
while the vehicle that transported them in life, their
body,
is reducing under that block of granite, dust back to
dust.

But if this be so, why will we not speculate beyond this
thought?
Why do we refuse to ask ourselves the question, gone
on to where?
To avoid this, we indulge in flights of fancy about the
"unknown."
However, the "unknown" is not unknown, quite the
contrary,
God, intentionally, very purposefully and I might add,
very mercifully,
provided us with a detailed and extensive revelation
on this subject.

Our merciful Creator inspired many men and women
by His Spirit
and over many centuries, to reveal manifest truth to
every man
on the larger issues of life, where did we come from,
why are we here,
is death the end and if not, where then do we go after
death?
The only infallible answers are revealed in God's Book,
the Bible,
if you will not read it, then to your ultimate dismay,
you will never know until it is too late.
I pray you will read the Bible and embrace Truth for
yourself.

Pleasant Thoughts

January 11, 2012

When worry beckons
Generate
Pleasant thoughts
That will relate
To peace on earth

For thoughts abhorrent
Germinate
Negativity and hate
For all they're worth

This object lesson
Indicates
The thought you choose
Facilitates
A change from gloom
To mirth

So choose this day
Good thoughts that may
Eradicate
Negativity and gloom
Then you will find that
Very soon

Gloom simply hasn't any room
To germinate

Each day awaken with a grin
Abandoning the old chagrin
Eternity you now will win
When choosing Christ for only He
Can cleanse your sin

My Vision's Beginning to Clear

September 10, 2012

If any man *come to me, and hate not his father, and mother, and wife, and children, and brethren, and sisters, yea, and his own life also, he cannot be my disciple.*

Luke 14:26

This commandment by Jesus, I could not equate,
it seemed quite contradictory.
For how could I hate,
those to whom I relate,
those most important in life to me.

For when I was young, my whole life had become
entangled by love for them all.
I loved dearly my mother,
my sister and brother,
and my dad as I clearly recall.

Now that I'm much older, a little more wise,
a new focus begins to appear.
As their numbers diminish,
and I'm nearing the finish,
my vision's beginning to clear.

My love for my Lord and my Savior's increasing,
in intensity more every day.
He's much more prominent,
I'm now wholly content,
as my family life's fading away.

So I now understand my Lord Jesus's command,
as the contrast comes into display.
If you're young, please don't fret,
you won't suffer regret,
when you too, begin fading away.

Pride-Humility

August, 2009

Must be careful I'm not throwing
stones at anyone for knowing
that my ugly pride is showing.
Glass houses shatter, so they say.

Retribution now is flowing,
Like winter weather when it's snowing.
Do I hear Satan near, hallowing,
pride can make one fall away.

You must pardon the foregoing,
is that my prideful horn I'm blowing,
to Satan my heart key bestowing,
excitement's leading me astray.

So I must now begin amending,
this wrong message I was sending,
pride caused me to be unbending,
I'll begin right now...today.

Must restore those I'm offending,
all those friendships I'm upending,
on Christianity depending,
which I must now display.

I'll no longer be defending
ugly pride, I'm now descending,
on this downward pathway wending.
Christ will lift me up... Hooray.

Humble yourselves in the sight of the Lord,
and he shall lift you up.
James 4:10

One World Religion

October 22, 2011

Peace, harmony, friendship
Solutions flouted by man
All of the world's religions
If they try, do you think they can
All join in one grand union
Love in men's hearts to abound
All of the hate to dissipate
As Jesus they seek to imitate
But where would truth be found
The heart is deceitful
Above all things
Desperately wicked too
How then, wicked hearts make pure
Not by wishing it so, for sure
Man's amalgamation would never endure
Something Jesus only can do
All men would have to die to self
Who would they then live to
Some false deceiver
From Satan's stealth
A quite indefinable stew
So peace on earth
Will only begin
When hearts of men
Are cleansed of sin

The Spirit of Christ
To dwell within
Every me and you

Rain Cycle

December 20, 2011

Invisibly, moisture sucks up to the sky,
as sun condenses the burnished sea
surrounding vast wastelands arid, dry,
where endless oceans of desert be.

Then borne away through heaven's expanse,
with moisture gathering into cloud
to join with others in riotous dance,
preparing a monsoon's watery shroud.

The cycles devolving, the waters fall,
some areas flooding perennially.
While others lie arid, no rain at all,
this always was, and it has to be.

For earth's heavenly sphere in its envelope,
spinning along with the water inside.
Every drop exists since creation spoke,
and the moon first tugged at the ocean's tide.

All forged into being that glorious day
when God spoke, and creation came to be.
Matters not, man's devises explain it away,
when God made the world, He made you and me.

Peace, Perfect Peace

December 3, 2012

In the place where God preserves memories
of the words, of the thoughts, of the deeds,
from the world of men, to refer to when
God's judgment on man proceeds.

What an ugly record would be amassed
from the hatred of man to man.
As they war and strive in the fight to survive,
just imagine it if you can.

But then in that place by God's pure grace,
residing there, shining bright.
Great records of beautiful acts of love
to fill God's heart with delight.

All of this is what Jesus our Lord surveyed
when He hung on the cross and cried.
When He paid the price for man's sin arrayed
and agreed to be crucified.

The day will come soon, when that evidence room
will once and forever be cleansed,
of each memory portending man's imminent doom,
after God's final judgments descend.

That day will then dawn, radiating upon
every man, sanctified and redeemed.
The goodness of God, all will gladly applaud,
perfect peace, ever hoped for and dreamed.

Spark of Glory

June 8, 2012

What source, that spark of glory in a man,
to utterly distinguish him from beast.
It must be real, since ere the world began,
man's lordship has alarmingly increased.

Observe the lion tamer in his cage,
manipulating savage tooth and claw.
When standing eye to eye, subdues the rage,
inherent in his Lordship's last hurrah.

That savage roar to paralyze with fear, the
helpless prey King Leo feeds upon.
Obsequiously though, lets man come near,
then backs away, turns tail to flee, is gone.

He could, with one gigantic leap obtain,
applying his superiority,
a man-sized meal with might and flowing mane,
what makes him bow, what causes him to flee.

The answer to this puzzle won't be found
in text book study or experiment.
It's in the Bible, mine's Morocco bound,
"subdue the world," to all the world's lament.

Perfection

May 30, 2011

Creation fire, God planted in man's heart, newly
unadorned
to slumber there, quite unaware of destiny.
While thoughts unbidden, lying hidden, upward
stormed,
to now and then break through the crust
of dumb, dark indifference, into creation's light to
thrust.
A revelation newly ordered from God's heart,
the numbing everyday routine to burst apart,
revealing to a newly opened mind, a glimpse of beauty
formed.
The petals of a flower bud that open to the oft
repeated
dance of life, so overheated, so divine, by God created
over time,
oft unseen to bloom away in some garden corner of
the wilderness.
And in this seeming carelessness of vast variety,
revealed,
whether seen or left unseen, it matters not,
God's generous explosion of colourful creation does
yet seem
to manifest a mass design occurring in a blink of time.

But Oh, so lovingly unique, each and every perfect
bloom
the Master's touch reveals, then each awakened heart
too soon
must sadly weep to witness such perfection's doom,
to perish after blessing God, the briefest afternoon.
And as with flowers, might not we also dare to say,
that God created every man in much the same
intentioned way.
And yes, man's beauty does apply, though some
require discerning eye,
for every heart that beats unseen, secretly must dare
to dream
eternity with God one day, to blossom in God's garden
in the sky.

Wine and Spirits

September 7, 2011

There's a hidden world around us
that cannot be seen or heard,
though the Bible speaks about it very much.
Most folks will not believe
that demon spirits could deceive,
for these spirits always stay just out of touch.

And that's the way the spirits like it,
shunning notoriety.
They don't want us to believe in them,
or recognise that each time when
they're influencing sinful men,
they really are attacking you and me.

Satan has a man for every woman
and a girl for every man.
When we choose to drink from Jesus's cup,
live righteous if we can.
We stir those dirty demons up,
they bring temptation to disrupt,
to make of you and I, an also ran.

For a whore is like a ditch that beckons, very deep,
a strange woman, not unlike a narrow pit.
She lieth there in wait for prey,
to cause transgression by the way,
our heart perverse in all we say
if we don't flee that trap, get out of it.

So we'd better pay attention for
temptation can be sweet,
forbidden fruit is tasty, awfully nice.
We must not tarry longer when the wine is fiery red,
it biteth like a serpent, we'd have demons in our bed,
and a mind consumed by alcohol and vice.

Perhaps this Poem Is Just for You

September 2, 2012

We come, we visit for a time,
but then, too soon we leave.
This world's been spinning like a top,
it's here to stay, will never stop,
if Bible truth thou choosest to believe.

But if thou choosest to deny
all Bible truth, may I ask why,
thou'rt privy to some evidence
that bodes to demonstrate more sense
to man who seekest God before he die.

To answer questions such as be,
why are we here, might puzzle thee.
Or questions like, where do we go,
to God above or hell below,
though you don't care, they surely interest me.

Thou canst believe this is the end,
much evidence doth sore contend
with that opinion, check it out, you'll see.
The Bible is inspired, divine,
I'll bet you've never spent the time
to study Bible evidence for free.

I don't know who I'm writing to,
perhaps this poem is just for you,
perhaps your heart is reaching out for love.
You owe it to yourself, my friend,
to read God's Word right to the end,
God loves you and He's watching from above.

The Colt

September 1, 2011

In a Galilean village on a sleepy afternoon,
I was resting in a shady by-the-way.
Because I knew he'd surely bolt,
I tied my yet unbroken colt
beside me, I was selling him today.

I was dreaming of a holy man, reputedly of late,
doing wonders and creating quite a din.
A stranger suddenly came by,
my colt, he started to untie,
bestirring me to rightly question him.

Because the Lord hath need of him, with a very
friendly grin,
my newfound friend, this explanation gave.
I felt I had to let him go,
the reason why, I'll never know,
I never even tried to stop the knave.

As he led my colt away, I knew I had to meet that day,
his master, and he happily agreed.
He led me to that Holy Man,
this Jesus who at once began,
to climb upon my unsuspecting steed.

Now I knew of the disaster that would happen to his
Master,
for that colt would never let him on his back.
We could not believe our eyes,
before we all could realize,
Jesus calmly rode away with halter slack.

Jesus Christ our Lord was praised by all with one
accord,
as they spread their clothes before Him in the way.
The man who owned the colt would tell
to everyone, and you as well,
about the miracle he saw that day,

Quench Not Thine Fire

August 21, 2012

If thou couldst find another heart so free,
a heart whose interest lay in thee alone.
Who self denies, who ever vies to see
thy joy fulfilled, thy life an ecstasy.

I pray thee, be thou noble this one time,
leave such a one unsullied by thy sin.
Destroy thee not, her happiness divine,
tiptoe away, a lesser heart to win.

Disturb her not, thy virgin do not touch,
such selfish ravaging, deny thine heart.
thou then wouldst be regarded overmuch
by Him whom sweet salvation doth impart.

Though, if thine heart be also pure and free,
with honourable intent, thy true desire.
Preferring yon sweet other, over any other,
God then wouldst bless thine union,
sanctified by church communion,
by God's mercy, wed the lady,
quench thine fire.

The Dance of Life

October 12, 2011

How swiftly flows the march of time,
how careless, each our portion use.
As on through life the hours chime,
no idle moment we refuse.

How unaware we spend the coin,
that fills the purse of life for each.
Though higher wisdom might enjoin,
though wiser teacher aptly teach.

The sand of time will endless flow,
each youthful heart will ever live.
Not caring where the hours go,
life freely won, time freely give.

The dance of life so gaily dance,
loves pleasures sweet, the spice of life.
The years go by as in a trance,
how harsh the drum, how sweet the fife.

And when the dance is finally done,
musicians leave and close up shop.
The dance must end for everyone,
as each in turn, the dancers drop.

Could we but stop the hour hand,
traversing round the face of time.
To dance without the music band,
grotesquely capering in mime.

That game not worth the candle, nay,
not doing anyone much good.
Sad candle, justly melts away,
pretending ends, as end it should.

But if we'll only learn to dance,
the dance that Jesus calls us to.
Commit to Jesus in advance,
we'll live forever, me and you.

Thank You, Lord

November 24, 2012

Dear God
Thank You for dragging me
Out of the mud
Thank You for washing off
All of the crud
Thank You for taking
The scales from my eyes
Thank You for clearing up
All of the lies
Thank You for revealing
That God is true
That the only true God
Can only be You
For letting me live
Long enough to know
There's a heaven above
And a hell below
That I will be Yours
For eternity
For eternity I
Will forever grow
In perfection's glow

Thought Life

January 11, 2012

When worry beckons
Generate
Pleasant thoughts
That will relate
To peace on earth

For thoughts abhorrent
Germinate
Negativity and hate
For all they're worth

This object lesson indicates
The thought you choose
Facilitates
A change from gloom
To mirth

So choose this day
Good thoughts that may
Eradicate
Negativity and gloom
Then you will find that
Very soon
Gloom simply hasn't any room
To germinate

The Gardener

July 17, 2011

A Lovely Soul, Christ grows but roses,
so hungry yet, though not for bread.
Deep in His heart desire reposes,
unfulfilled, and as one supposes,
Spirit led.

Sustained with food we know not of,
His hunger be not of this world.
Eternally birthed in heaven above,
expressed in the bud of a rose's love,
unfurled.

And as this gentle Life grows dim,
His flowers beautify.
The world is lovely because of Him,
with bounty flowing down from within
God's sky.

And though departed, He still is here,
as His gardens testify.
If you seek Him true, He will be found,
just listen close, let love abound,
don't pass Him by.

True Prosperity

August 8, 2011

It's great to garner extra cash
to pile atop my growing stash,
soon I'll have enough to last,
Prosperity!

Soon time to bid a fond adieu,
there's really nothing we can do
As death approaches me and you,
So Terribly!

And when at last, we write finis,
our exit from this world will be
the entrance grand for us to see
The Heavenly!

Where then we all will give account to God,
not of our cash amount,
but what we did with Jesus Christ,
You See!

Where our treasure is, our heart will be,
So our only true prosperity,
is embracing Christianity,
You and Me!

Ambition's Condition

October 16, 2009

How oft through life, we lovers of acclaim,
pretenders to fame's throne would ever seek
for office high, the common life disdain,
be strong tho' vulgar, sophist, never meek.

To clamber over others in the way,
ambition slake with approbation from our peers.
These weak competitors with feet of clay,
who hesitate, then fail because of fears.

Not I, my lad, to be the one to flag,
to falter or to favor others who
through weakness or distraction catch a snag,
no time to stop and help, too much to do.

Through woodland bounding, heard no sounding of
alarm,
unaware that God is there, to intercept
this blind and callow fellow, lacking charm,
bereft of all life's graces, so inept.

In these woodland bowers, sunny flowers
all surround him with the laughter of the Lord.
His eyes are opened as he loiters there for hours
with boyhood memories of the joy of God's accord.

His hardened heart now comes apart with many tears,
remembering long ago his Mother's prayers,
those shining hours in Mother's arms secure from
fears,
to fall asleep and then be carried up the stairs.

The Son comes shining through in flowered sylvan
glade,
our candidate immersed, must slake his thirst, for
God.
Sin belying, hastens flying to right the wrongs he
made,
our transformed one with winged gospel, feet now
shod.

While up in heaven, sweet Treleven, Mother dear,
peering over edge of heaven, Oh so brave.
A Mother's prayers are truly answered, redemption
clear.
Great rejoicing angels voicing, for this sinner truly
saved.

Urgent Pertinacity

February 11, 2012

Ah, Lord! Would that such a one as I
might speak to thee words ever wise.
But I must feign be limit by
the words a simple man devise,
which nothing more imply.

To never prate upon a word
like importunity.
To speak thus would seem quite absurd,
a word that's hardly ever heard,
in interfaith community.

For if my words were importune,
expressed with urgent rudeness.
I'm sure I would not be immune,
from retribution very soon,
to punish my intrudeness.

But then in Luke 11:8
the seeker after bread.
Did speak with importunity,
receiving bread, and then I read
proceeded with immunity.

And so, my Lord, thy word implies
that You will hear our plea.
To quickly meet our urgent need,
if we are not expressing greed,
with urgent pertinacity.

Creation of Man

May, 2009

Have you ever considered the enormity of,
the reality of man's creation.
Do you think that, once the first model was made,
and given animation,
some divine cookie-cutter stamps us out,
to create everyone we're seeing.
Duplicating the perfect complexity,
of just your physical being.

Oh no! This simplistic assessment of,
the supreme creation of man.
This physical mystery, just in itself,
exposes a purposeful plan.
To accommodate the many unknowns,
this simple reflection reveals,
far deeper realities must be faced,
how man functions, creates, and feels.

The part of a man that's simplest by far,
is his physical house, his abode. Scientists compete to
be the star,
to crack man's genetic code.

Will they build their cookie-cutter,
will they be cloning man for sure, will
we one day hear world scientists say,
"we now have every cure"?

But let's think of for now, the reality how,
each body possesses a soul,
the emotional, thinking, feeling part,
without this, man wouldn't be whole.
And then there's the spirit, the essence of life,
that God breathed into man.
In conclusion it's true, God created you,
Spirit, Soul, and body...God's plan.

*And the LORD God formed man of the dust of the
ground, and breathed into his nostrils
the breath of life; and man became a living soul.*
Genesis 2:7

Where Dwellest Thou

June 23, 2012

Come spirit man, why hideth thou within
Reveal thyself, let thou and I begin
That we might'st come together in a way
To benefit each other well this day
Reveal thyself, for surely thou dost see
I needest thou, just as thou needest me
For I afford thee carriage on thy way
Thus otherwise immobile thou wouldst stay
Whilst thou affordest me thy vision grand
Advantaging my soul quite out of hand
This day a Bible clue didst haply find
To prove thou dwellest not within my mind
From out my belly lying fold on fold
Dost flow God's living waters, I was told
So there I do suspect, thou dost reside
Reclined in well fed solitude inside
Mayhap if I might look inside I'd see
Thy lodging where reclining thou dost be
Where then mayhap thy door might open wide
Affording me safe passaging inside
Where we'd recline together, just we three
Body, soul, and spirit whole
Whilst sharing covertly, three cups of tea
Then hopefully, thou openly with me wouldst share
God's great eternal secrets earthward flown

Whilst we contentedly are fellowshipping there
Alas, for now intrudes this thought, so searing hot
For me to know as even I am known
God needest urgently forthwith, to slay me on the spot

All Is Not Lost

August 12, 2011

The struggles of man with tomorrow's sorrows,
temptations ever begun.
Trapped in the sins of the flesh unaware
of eternal damnation lurking there
as we break God's commandments without a care
for the reckoning soon to come.

With pride of life we fantasize
the lust of the flesh and lust of the eyes
deceiving everyone.
Satisfaction we never will realize,
false visions can never materialize
in this race forever run.

Deception is Satan's stock in trade
as he offers this rosy glow.
Extending to all, a succulent treat,
which becomes a lemon instead of a peach,
then seems to forever be out of reach,
of us sinners here below.

So what can we do, it seems all is lost
for sinners with Satan enmeshed.
But all is not lost if we'll follow the way
offered by God in his Word today,
with Satan and sin, no longer play,
seek Christ for a life refreshed.

Why Am I Here?

May 31, 2011

Why am I here? Tell me, why am I here?
Though I don't have an answer, the question's quite
clear.
Well, I'm here for my family, I'm here to enjoy
the sports on T.V., see the skill they employ.
But that can't be the reason, that's not very deep,
Can it be for the beer and the work and the sleep?
I do favour the beer, not the work I employ,
and I never can get all the sleep I enjoy.
Hey! I'm here for the weekends, though they never last,
am I here to watch summer vacations fly past?
Now I know why I'm here, for retirement to come,
I'll have time to recline, get to know everyone.
But retirement will end, then what will I do,
when I finally know, him and her, me and you?
What then is the point, we'll all die anyway,
I'm back where I started, now what can I say?
Why would I ever go through all that living,
when I'll end up a corpse and what's left I'll be giving
back to the earth, I hear that's where I'm from,
with no one to care if I go or I come.
What's that you say, there is someone who cares,
One who's watching me now and knows all my affairs?
He loves me and wants me? That's hard to believe,
He's the reason for wearing my heart on my sleeve?

Hey! If this is all true, then please count me in,
I'm as green as the grass, don't know where to begin.
You say all have sinned, come short of His glory,
if I acknowledge my sinfulness, tell Him I'm sorry,
my soul He will save, then I'll know that the grave,
will never, forever, end my life's story?
So this is God's reply, to the question I asked,
it's Jesus my Saviour, my answer at last.

Four Horsemen
May 25, 2012

Put your ear to the ground,
what you'll hear is the sound
of a thunderous stampeding horde.
Four horsemen, apocalyptic they say,
for thousands of years they have stayed away,
but they now are unsheathing the sword.

And the reason we're in
this condition, is sin,
to deny it won't do any good.
The warnings outlined in the Bible are sure,
from the heart of our God who is righteous and pure,
liberating, when they're understood.

From our God who is Sovereign, with rule over all,
a white horse appears charging, pay heed to his call
as rampaging forth he goes.
For he carries a bow,
symbolism we know
of conquest, to all who oppose.

A black horse appears next, with a warning to tell
of a famine consuming all those who rebel,
and with no place for any to hide.

Populations from hunger
kill, steal without number
as armies with armies collide.

A pale horse is next, summarising in kind,
his rider is Death, Hades not far behind
with power, much people to kill.
Precursors they are
of destruction by far
much worse, that is coming still.

This is really a message from God to us all
for repentance, if only we'll answer His call
and acknowledge His sovereignty.
For Christ went to the cross
to deliver from loss,
every sinner, that's you and that's me!

Why Animals

February 19, 2011

Why do animals exist on this orbiting sphere,
to eat or be eaten, is that why they're here?
Why the striving, competing, from birth until death,
then not long after taking their very last breath,
they're inspected, dissected, fat content corrected,
and they do taste delicious, my dear.

All the animals function by thoughtless instinct,
no self-discerning, no yearning to think.
They survive in life meeting each physical need,
motivated by self-preservation or greed.
They appear, reproduce, stay awhile and then scram,
no missing link left between monkeys and man.

While we, on the other hand, live to create,
examine, enquire, or excel in debate.
Our rocket ships take us from here over there,
submarine in the ocean, then come up for air.
Or we organize games, even travel in trains,
things monkeys cannot imitate.

We are not just like animals, plainly I see,
we're created uniquely, my friends, you and me.
In the Bible account of creation of old,
vegetation would adequately feed us we're told,

when God graciously purposed to walk among men,
as He will when He visits this planet again.

There will be no more death in that wondrous day,
all the animals no longer need run away.
We won't kill and prepare them as barbecued ribs,
in that very soon day, we'll stop eating their kids.
So I now understand what the Good Lord intends,
He desires them and us to again become friends.

Adultery

July 19, 2011

The elegant frame
of a beautiful dame,
might cause a man to sin.

He need not repair
to a room somewhere,
this lovely lady and him.

For that sin, you see,
could catch you or me,
if our mind inclined within.

For the sin transpired
when the thought was fired,
to stretch a synonym.

If you doubt my word,
if it seems absurd,
it's from an impeccable source.

The Bible speaks true,
it's for me and you,
and all seekers of truth, of course.

In Matthew 5:28,
we adulterate,
when envisioning lust within.

If we lust in our heart,
that is only the start,
to a life of willful sin.

Remember Me

May 2, 2011

Remember me as one who cares,
who took the bitter with the sweet.
Ne'er meddled in a friend's affairs,
nor ever needed to compete.

Remember me a faithful friend,
this treader of the mortal sod.
Who joyfully through life did wend,
who ever bent the knee to God.

Remember me as one who loved,
perhaps too oft, but God would know.
With tenderness, all else above,
who'd tread where brave men feared to go.

Remember me as spirit blithe,
who squandered love with great aplomb.
Who loved indeed, each loving wife,
and did until God called me home.

Recall me not as profligate,
but rather, one who loved to bless.
To loose displaying ne'er relate,
to parsimony even less.

But most of all, please do recall,
my poetry with style and wit.
Remember me as one who left,
a legacy of godly writ.

Look for other volumes from
poet Bob McCluskey's prolific pen:

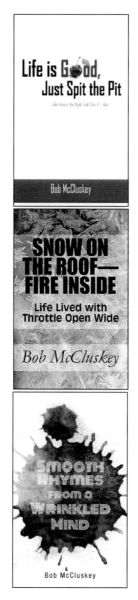